ROCK GU PHOTO CHORDS

BY COREY CHRISTIANSEN

MW01201523

1 2 3 4 5 6 7 8 9 0

Visit us on the Web at www.melbay.com — E-mail us at email@melbay.com

2

Table of Contents

Introduction

Rock Guitar Photo Chords is a streamlined way for beginners to learn the most commonly used rock chords. Many of these chords are moveable shapes. This means that by knowing the names of the notes on the fretboard, the shapes presented can be played in virtually every key. The concept of moveable chords is invaluable for all guitarists. It allows us to learn a single shape, and by moving that shape around the fretboard, the chord can be played in every key. All you need to know is where the root (the note that names the chord) is. Page 24 has diagrams that will help you understand the layout of the fretboard. We're not going to show you every possible chord in this book, but if you understand the concept of the moveable chord, you can fill in the missing pieces. Be sure to learn each shape not only in the single key presented, but in all twelve keys. You will not only learn 12 times more chords, but learn the layout of the fretboard. There will be some information on how this is done throughout the book. Most importantly, the book presents each chord in standard notation, tab, a fretboard diagram and with a photo of how it is fingered. This presentation covers all the bases making these chords very easy to learn. Have fun using all of these chords.

How to Use This Book

Below are explanations for the fretboard diagrams and tab that are used in the book. Standard notation and photos are also used to help students learn what notes are used in each chord and to help them see what the chord literally looks like when played on the guitar.

With the chord diagrams, the vertical lines represent the strings on the guitar, with the first string being on the right. The horizontal lines represent frets, with the first fret being on the top. Dots, or numbers, on the lines show the placement of left-hand fingers. The numbers on, or next to the dots indicate which left-hand finger to use. A diamond may be used to indicate the placement of the root of the chord or scale. **Root** refers to a note which has the same letter name as the chord or scale.

A zero above the string indicates the string is to be played open (no left-hand fingers are pushing on the string. An "X" above a string indicates that the string is not to be played, or that the string is to be muted by tilting one of the left-hand fingers and touching the string lightly.

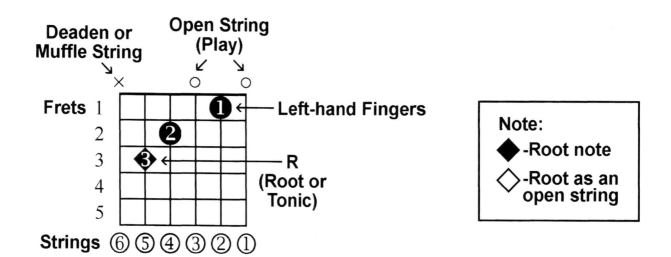

Tablature

One way of writing guitar music is called tablature. The six horizontal lines represent the strings on a guitar. The top line is the first string. The other strings are represented by the lines in descending order as shown below.

A number on a line indicates in which fret to place a left-hand finger.

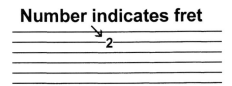

In the example below, the finger would be placed on the first string in the third fret.

1st String, 3rd Fret

If two or more numbers are written on top of one another, play the strings at the same time.

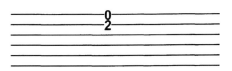

Open Chords

Open chords are the most commonly used chords in the world. They are used in virtually every style of music. They are called open chords because they utilize open strings (strings that are not fingered). Most of these types of chords are in first position. This means that the first four frets of the guitar (and mostly just the first three frets) are used to execute these chords.

Open Chords

C

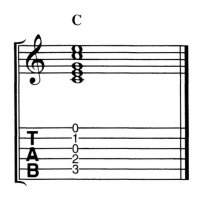

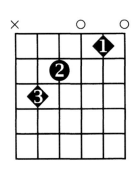

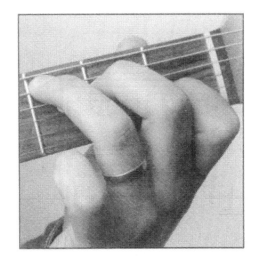

C Maj7

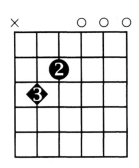

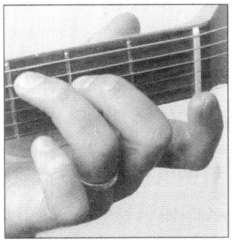

C 7

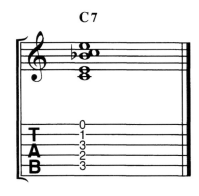

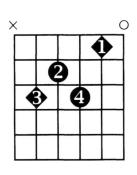

C 6

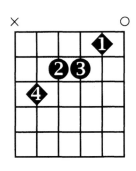

Open Chords

G

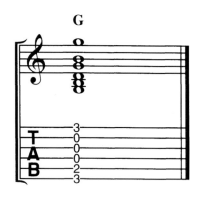

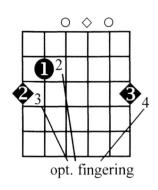

opt. fingering

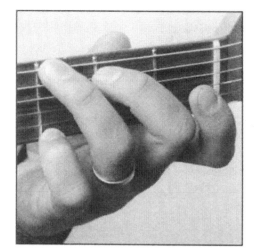

G

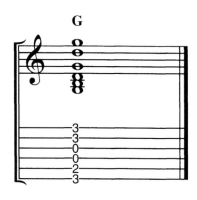

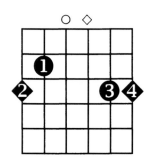

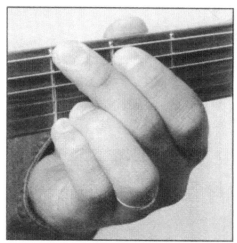

G Maj7

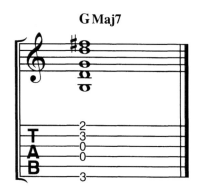

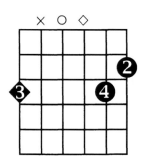

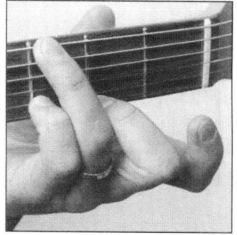

G 7

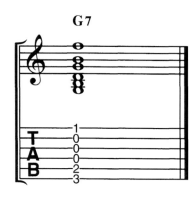

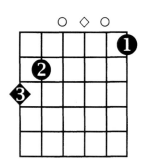

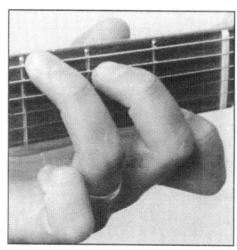

8

Open Chords

D

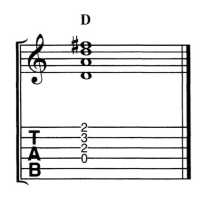 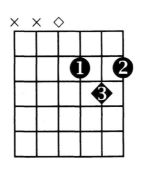 

D Maj7

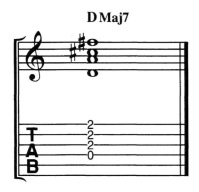 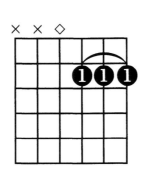 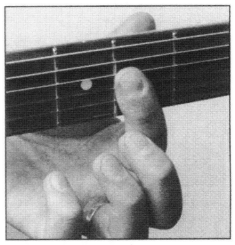

D 7

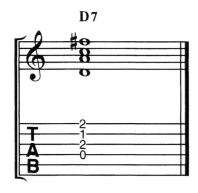 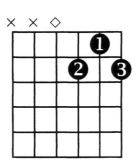 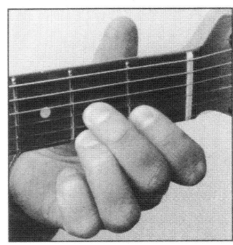

Open Chords

D m

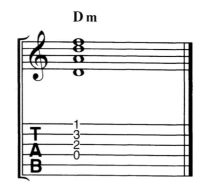

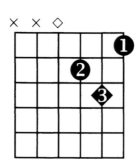

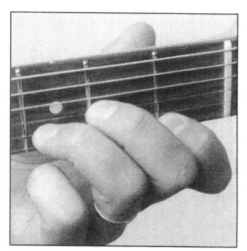

D m7

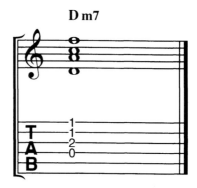

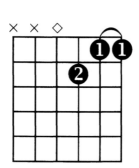

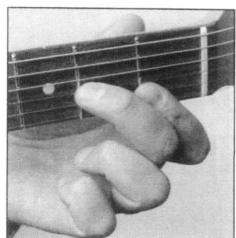

Open Chords

A

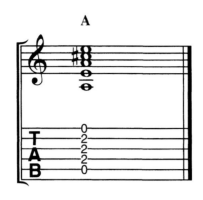

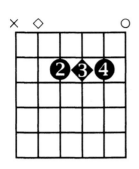

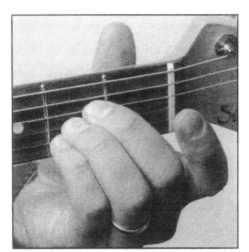

A Maj7

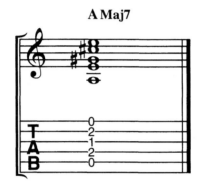

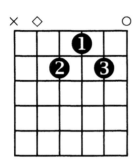

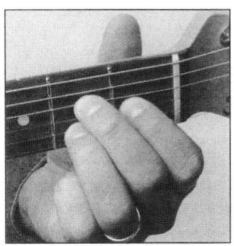

A 7

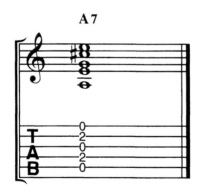

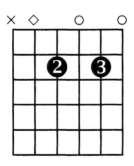

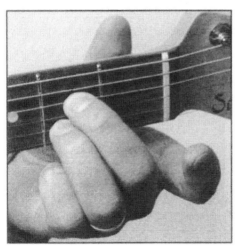

Open Chords

A m

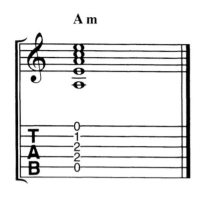

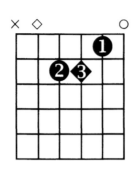

A m7

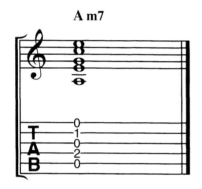

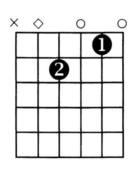

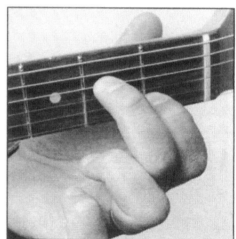

A m7

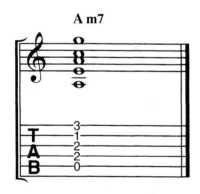

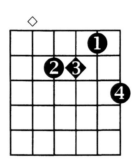

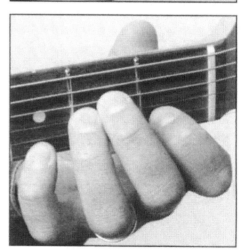

Open Chords

E

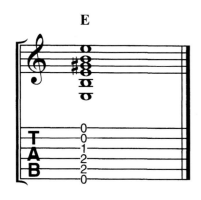

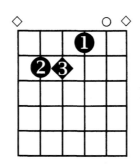

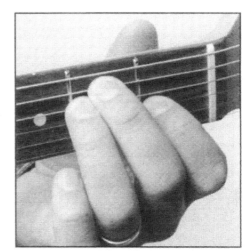

E 7

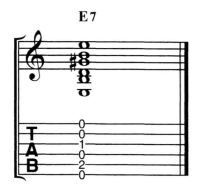

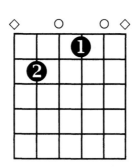

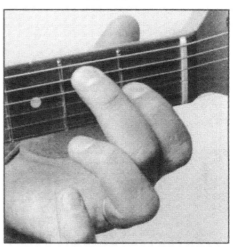

E m

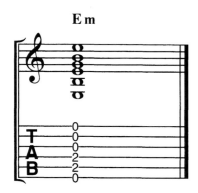

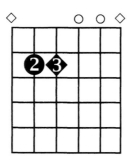

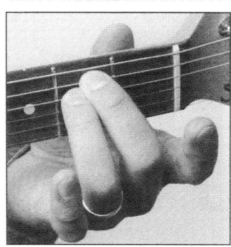

Open Chords

E m7

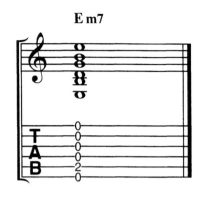 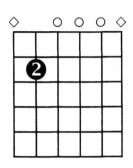 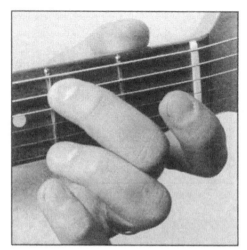

E m7

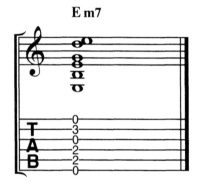 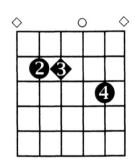 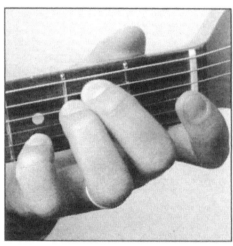

B 7

 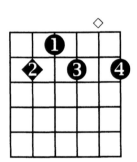 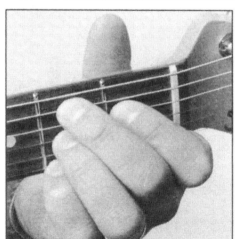

Open Add9 (sus2) Chords

Cadd9

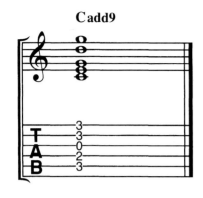

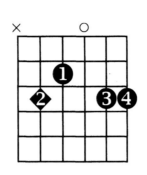

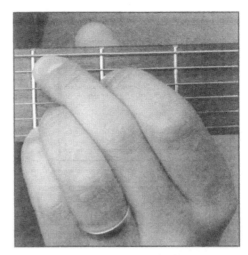

Gadd9

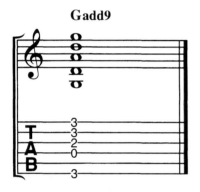

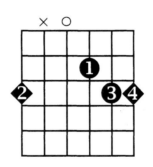

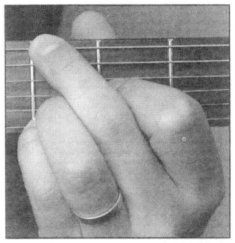

Dadd9

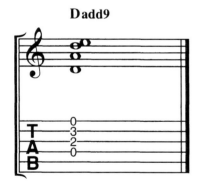

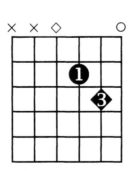

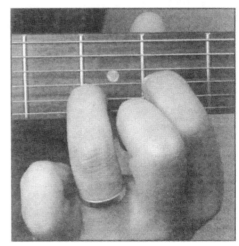

Open Add9 (sus2) Chords

A add9

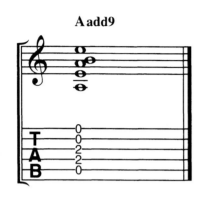

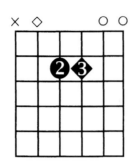

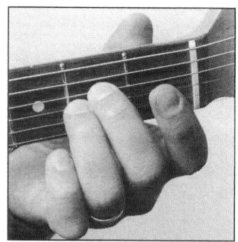

E add9

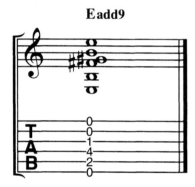

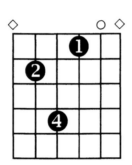

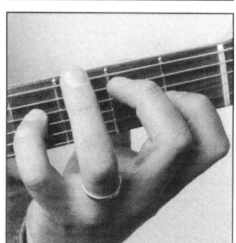

Open Suspended (sus4 or sus) Chords

C sus4

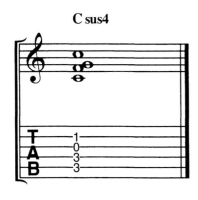
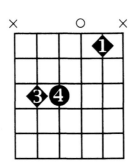
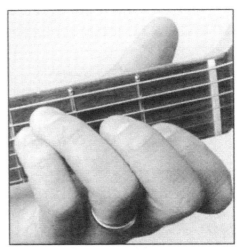

C sus4

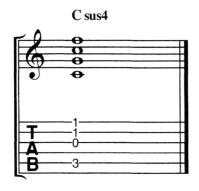
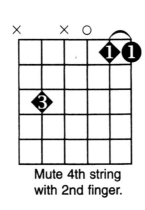

Mute 4th string
with 2nd finger.

C sus4

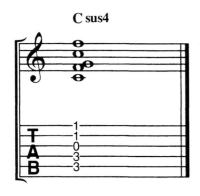
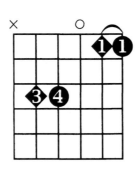
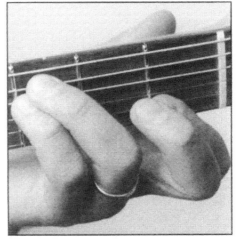

G sus4

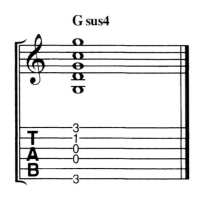
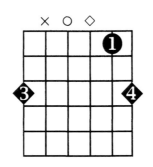
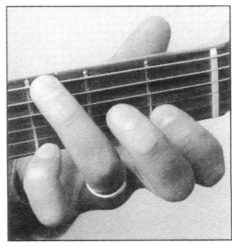

Open Suspended (sus4 or sus) Chords

D sus4

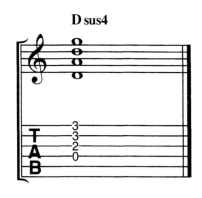
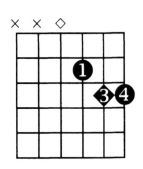

A sus4

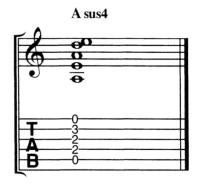
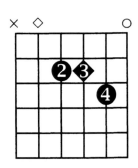
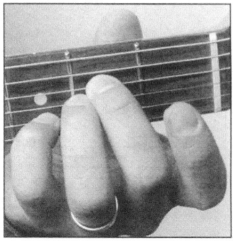

E sus4

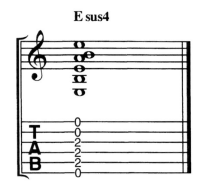
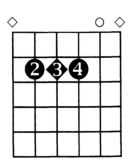
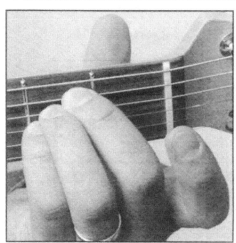

Power Chords

Power chords are the backbone of rock 'n roll. They are heavy sounding chords that are easily played and work in many settings. They are most commonly referred to as "5" chords. Therefore E5 is the same as saying, "E power chord."

Open Power Chords

E5

 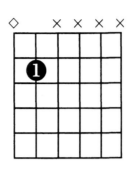 

E5

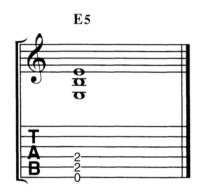 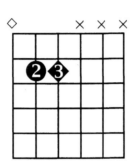 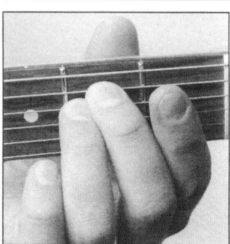

Open Power Chords

A5

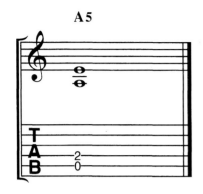

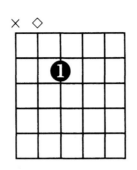

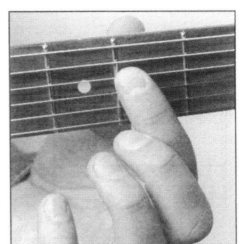

A5

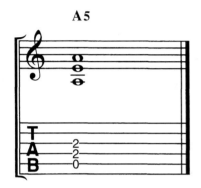

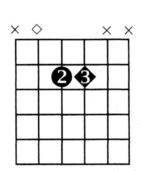

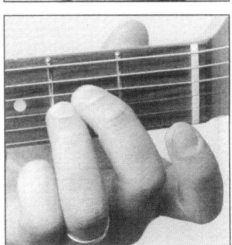

Open Power Chords

D 5

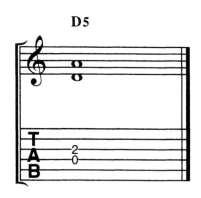

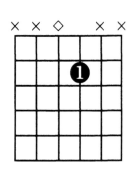

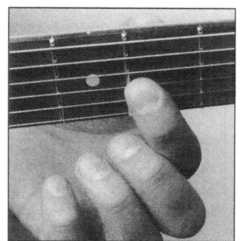

D 5

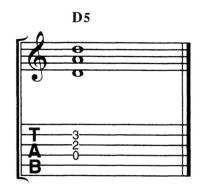

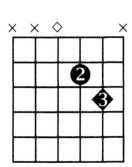

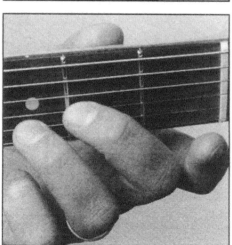

Add the Sixth

A common variation on the power chord involves adding a finger on the third and seventh down-strokes (on the second and fourth beats) of the measure. For example, on the A5 chord, play strings 5 and 4 together four times. Use only down-strokes. On the third stroke, add the left-hand third finger where the "3" is drawn on the diagram below. On the fourth stroke, lift the third finger. Do this twice in each measure.

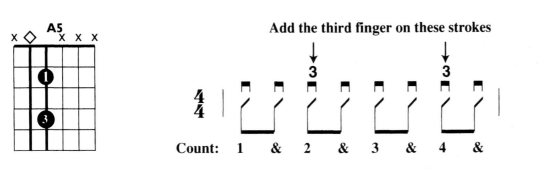
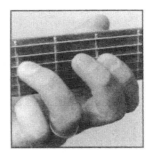

This technique could be used on the D5 chord by adding the third finger on the third string where the "3" is drawn.

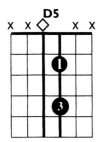
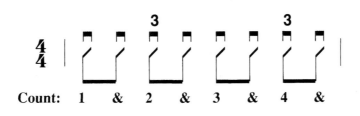

For the E5, add the third finger in the fourth fret on the fifth string.

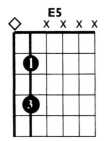
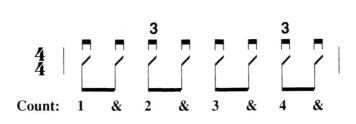
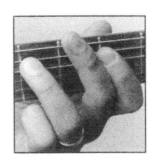

Play this twelve-bar blues which uses the variations on the power chord.

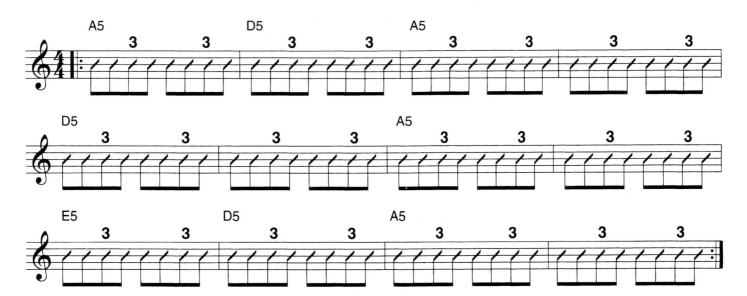

Moveable Power Chords

Moveable chords are great because they can be played in any key, and are usually lumped into a few groups. The first group are shapes based off the root note (note that names the chord) on the sixth string. The second is based off shapes with the root on the fifth string and the third group is based off shapes with the root on the fourth string. Of course, the root can be on any string for moveable chords. Whatever fret the root note is placed in will determine the name of the chord. Diagrams showing the root notes on all of the strings are found below. Remember to flat (♭) a note, lower it (move it closer to the headstock of the guitar) by one fret. To sharp (♯) a note, raise it (move it closer to the body of the guitar) by one fret. The first type of moveable chord shapes are moveable power chords. Be sure to practice these chords in all twelve keys. Notice there are three shapes for some of these chords. One has the root on the lowest sounding string, one has two root notes, and the other has the root on the highest sounding string.

Root Notes on the Sixth String

Fret	0	1	3	5	7	8	10	12
Root Name	E	F	G	A	B	C	D	E

Root Notes on the Fifth String

Fret	0	2	3	5	7	8	10	12
Root Name	A	B	C	D	E	F	G	A

Root Notes on the Fourth String

Fret	0	2	3	5	7	9	10	12
Root Name	D	E	F	G	A	B	C	D

Notes on the 3rd String

0	2	4	5	7	9	10	12
G	A	B	C	D	E	F	G

Notes on the 2nd String

0	1	3	5	6	8	10	12
B	C	D	E	F	G	A	B

Notes on the 1st String

0	1	3	5	7	8	10	12
E	F	G	A	B	C	D	E

Moveable Power Chords

Root Based on 6th String

A5

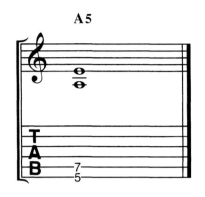

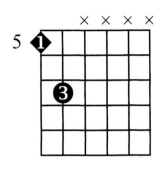

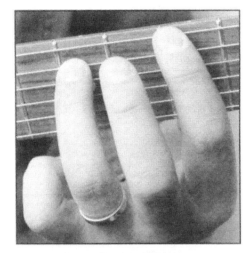

A5

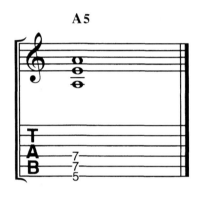

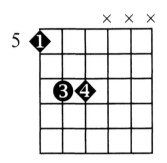

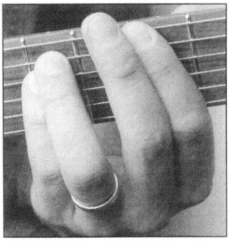

A5

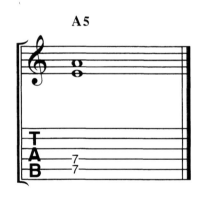

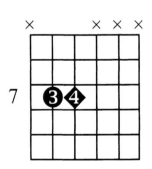

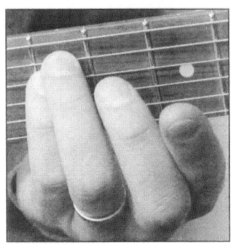

Note: the chords on this page are moveable and can be played
in any of the twelve keys. See page 24 for more information.

Moveable Power Chords
Root Based on 5th String

D5

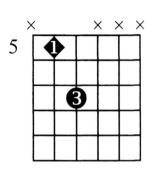
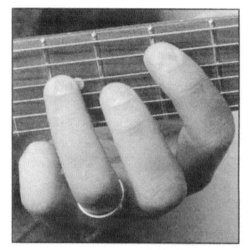

D5

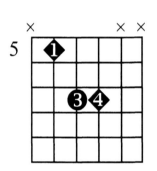
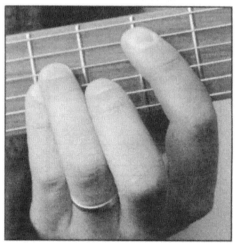

D5

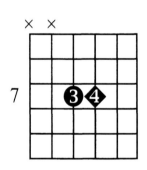
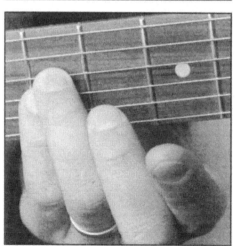

Note: the chords on this page are moveable and can be played
in any of the twelve keys. See page 24 for more information.

Moveable Power Chords

Root Based on 4th String

G5

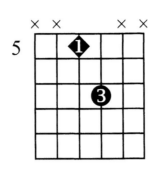

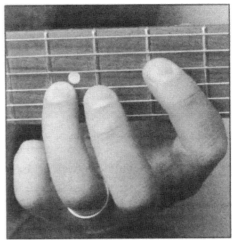

G5

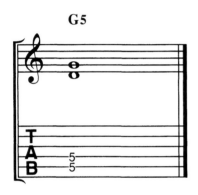

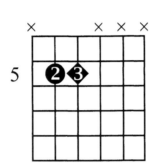

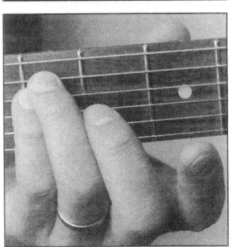

Note: the chords on this page are moveable and can be played
in any of the twelve keys. See page 24 for more information.

Barre Chords

Like moveable power chords, barre chords are moveable shapes. They are called barre chords because at least one finger is used to press down more than one string at a time. The following chords have their roots on the sixth string and the fifth string.

6th String Barre Chords
Root on 6th String

G Major

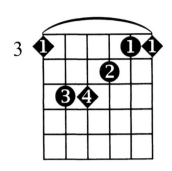

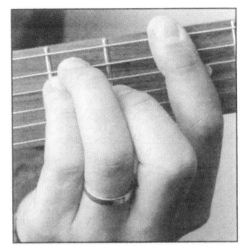

G m

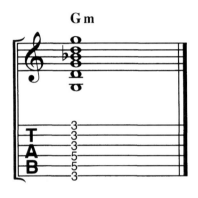

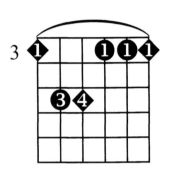

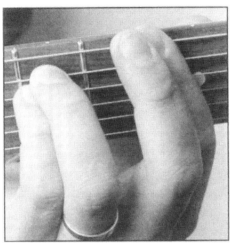

G 7

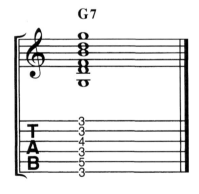

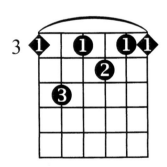

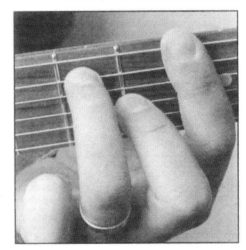

G m7

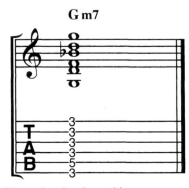

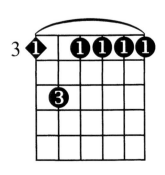

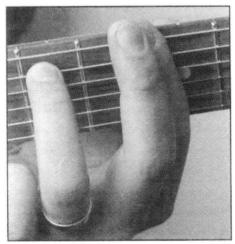

Note: the chords on this page are moveable and can be played
in any of the twelve keys. See page 24 for more information.

6th String Barre Chords
Root on 6th String

G m7

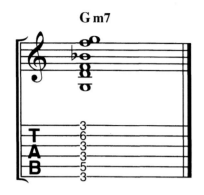

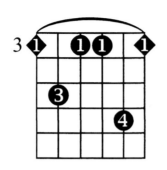

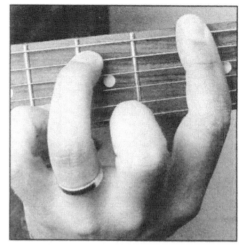

G sus4

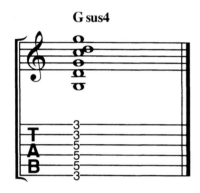

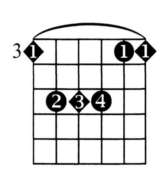

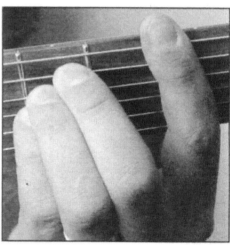

G 7sus4

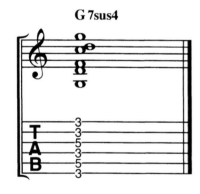

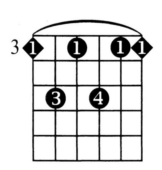

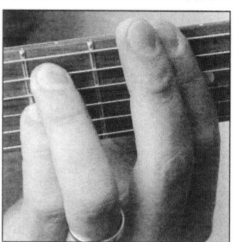

Note: the chords on this page are moveable and can be played
in any of the twelve keys. See page 24 for more information.

Root on 5th String

C

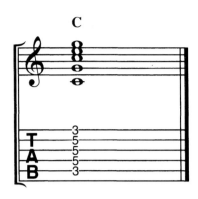

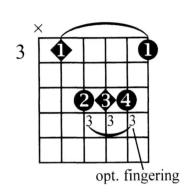

opt. fingering

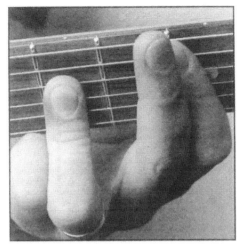

Cm

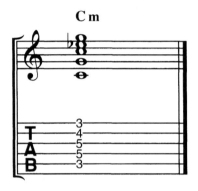

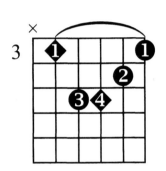

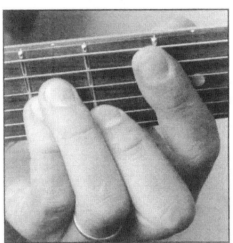

C7

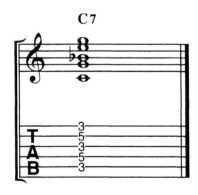

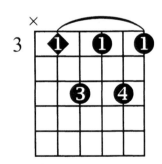

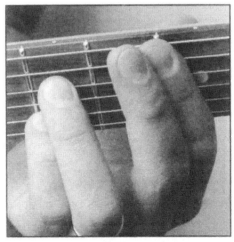

Cm7

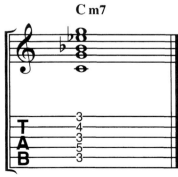

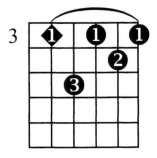

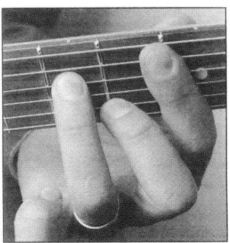

Note: the chords on this page are moveable and can be played in any of the twelve keys. See page 24 for more information.

5th String Barre Chords
Root on 5th String

C sus4

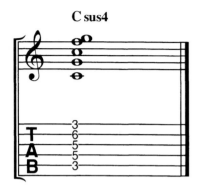 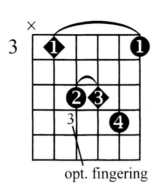

opt. fingering

C 7sus4

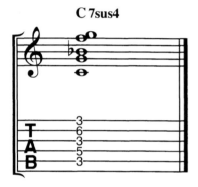 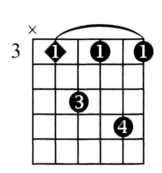

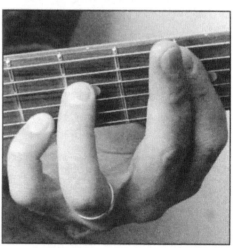

CMaj7

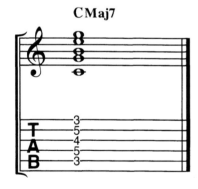 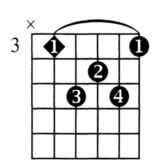

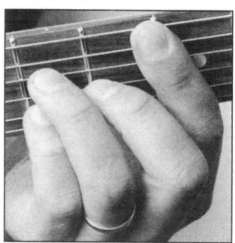

Note: the chords on this page are moveable and can be played
in any of the twelve keys. See page 24 for more information.

Four-String Chords

Four-string chords can be used in a variety of settings. They are the perfect choice when a lighter sound is desired. They also work great when playing with another guitarist. Rather than doubling the exact same G chord in open position, for example, the four-string chord with the same name can be used. It creates the sound of a much larger chord. Groups with more than one guitar have used this concept to create some wonderful guitar orchestrations.

Notice that some of the chords are written with a slash. This means that a note other than the root note is in the lowest position. This is called an inversion. It is still the same chord, just a different organization or order of the notes. These chords can really sound great when used correctly. All of these chords are presented with G as the root note. Be sure to practice these in many other keys as well.

For each chord, at least two inversions are presented. The inversions are indicated by a slash (G/B). In the case of G/B, this means G with B in the bass.

Four-String Chords
Major

G

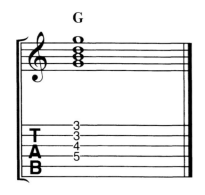

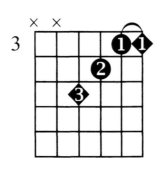

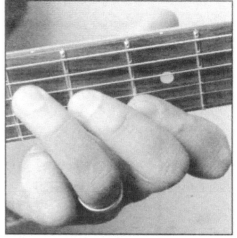

G/B

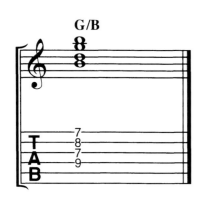

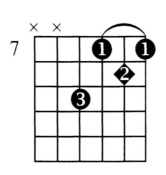

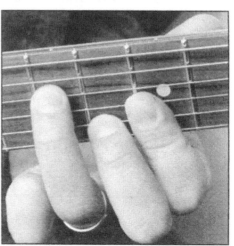

G/D

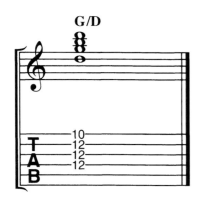

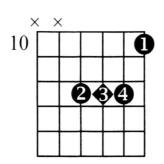

Note: the chords on this page are moveable and can be played in any of the twelve keys. See page 24 for more information.

Four-String Chords
Minor

G m

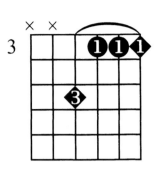

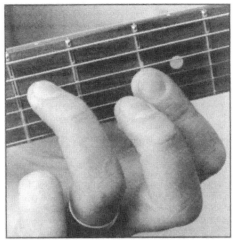

G m/B♭

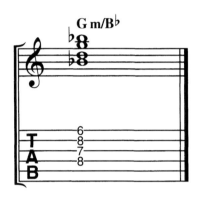

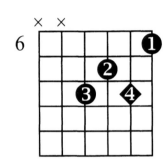

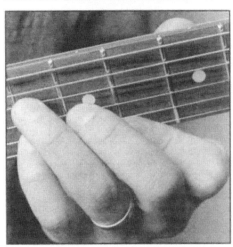

G m/D

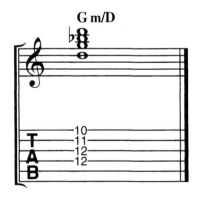

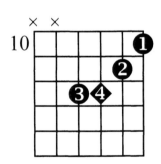

Note: the chords on this page are moveable and can be played
in any of the twelve keys. See page 24 for more information.

Four-String Chords
Major 7th

GMaj7/F#

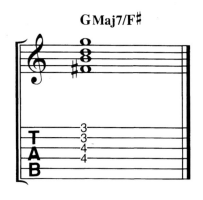

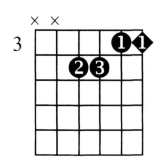

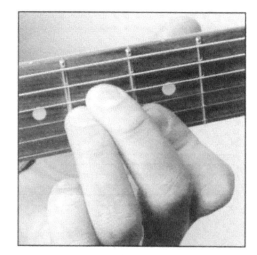

GMaj7

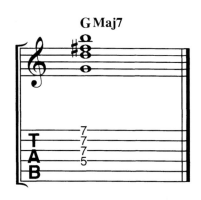

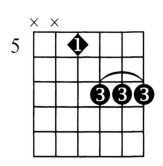

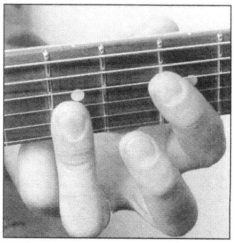

GMaj7/B

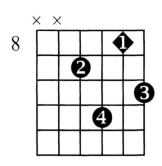

GMaj7/D

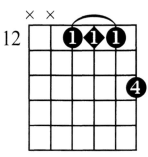

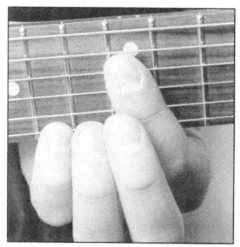

Note: the chords on this page are moveable and can be played in any of the twelve keys. See page 24 for more information.

Four-String Chords

Dominant 7th

G 7/F

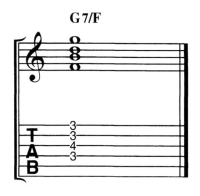

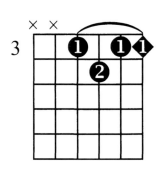

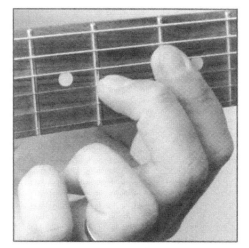

G 7

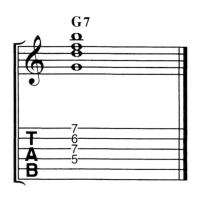

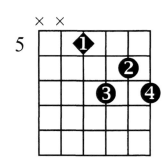

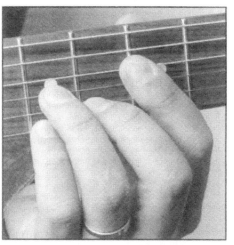

G 7/B

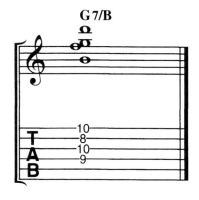

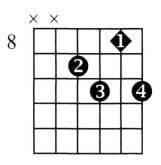

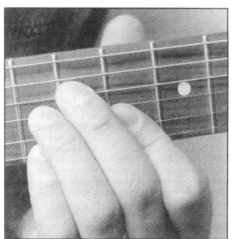

G 7/D

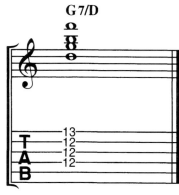

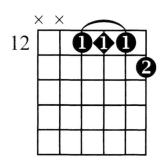

Note: the chords on this page are moveable and can be played
in any of the twelve keys. See page 24 for more information.

Four-String Chords
6th

G 6/E

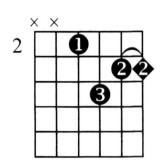

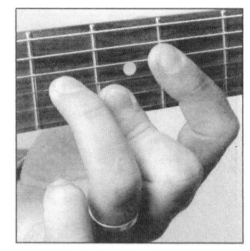

G 6

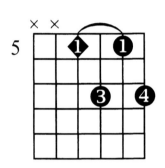

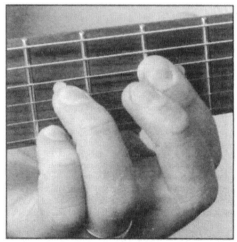

G 6/B

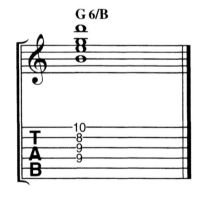

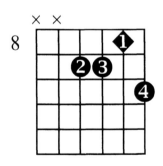

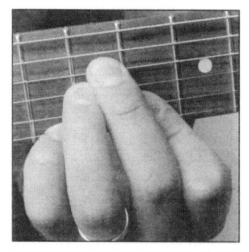

G 6/D

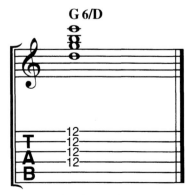

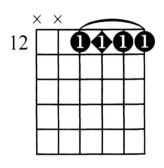

Note: the chords on this page are moveable and can be played
in any of the twelve keys. See page 24 for more information.

Four-String Chords
Minor 7th

G m7/F

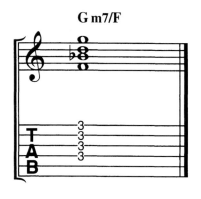

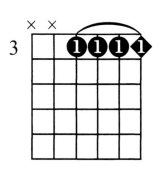

3

G m7

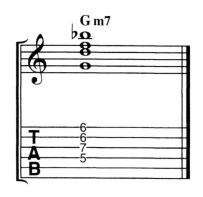

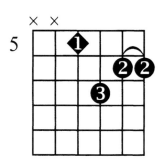

5

G m7/B♭

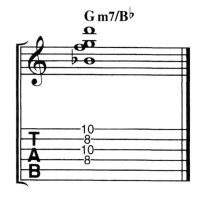

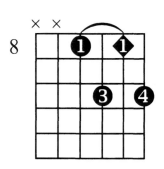

8

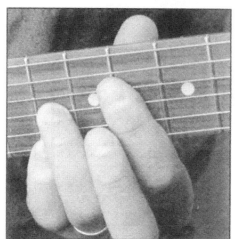

G m7/D

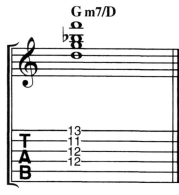

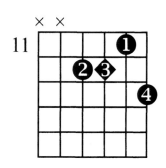

11

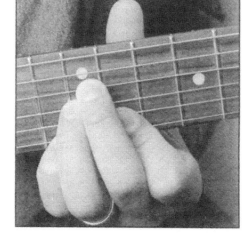

Note: the chords on this page are moveable and can be played
in any of the twelve keys. See page 24 for more information.

Four-String Chords
Minor 6th

G m6/E

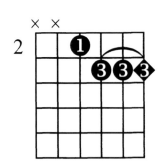
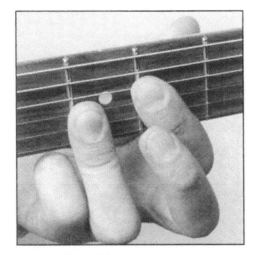

G m6

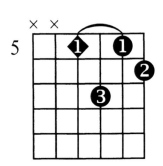
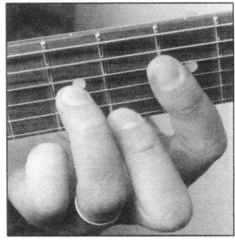

G m6/B♭

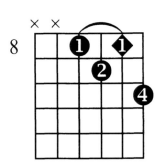

G m6/D

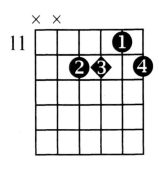
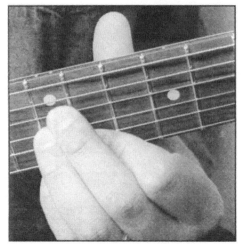

Note: the chords on this page are moveable and can be played in any of the twelve keys. See page 24 for more information.

Four-String Chords

Minor 7(♭5)

G m7(♭5)/F

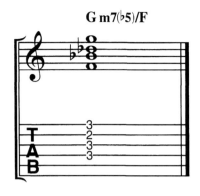

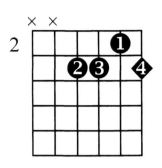

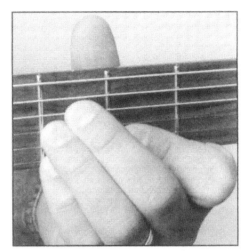

G m7(♭5)

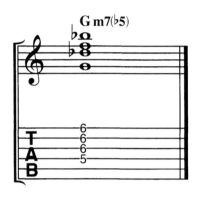

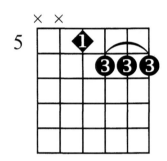

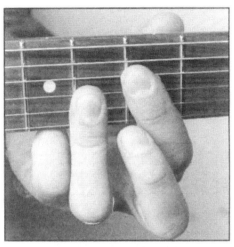

G m7(♭5)/B♭

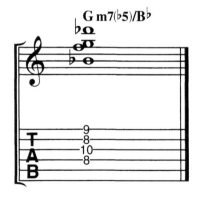

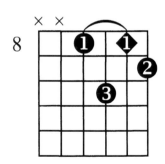

G m7(♭5)/D♭

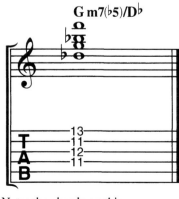

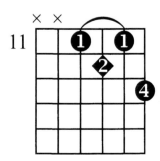

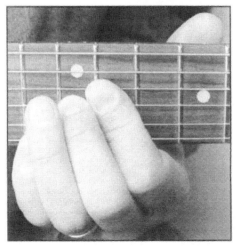

Note: the chords on this page are moveable and can be played in any of the twelve keys. See page 24 for more information.

Four-String Chords

Diminished 7th

G dim7/E

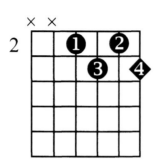

G dim7

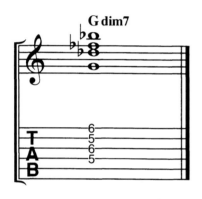

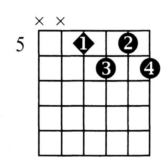

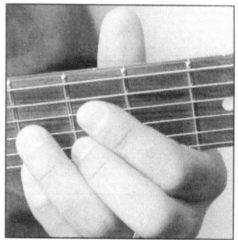

G dim7/B♭

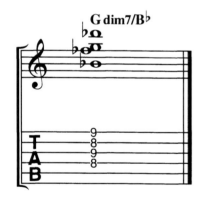

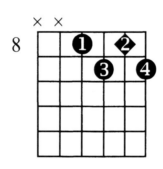

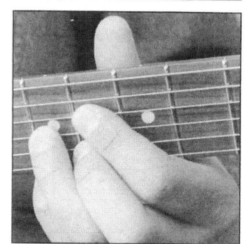

G dim7/D♭

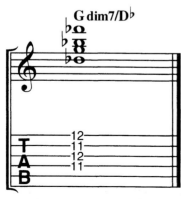

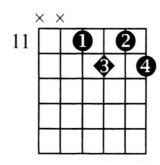

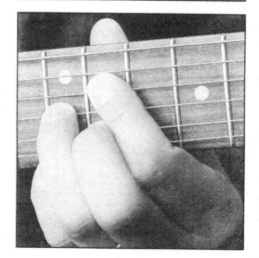

Note: the chords on this page are moveable and can be played in any of the twelve keys. See page 24 for more information.

Other Moveable Chords

The following are other moveable chords that are used in rock music. Enjoy!

Other Moveable Chords

Gadd9

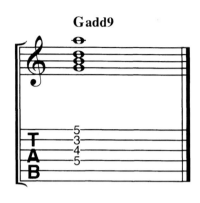

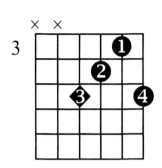

Gadd9

Play the low G with
the left-hand thumb.

Thumb

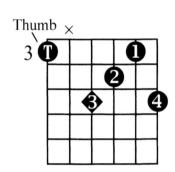

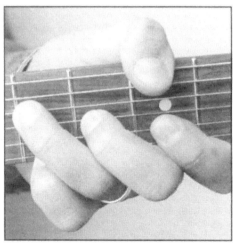

C 9

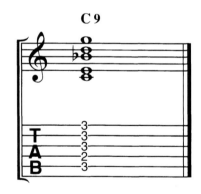

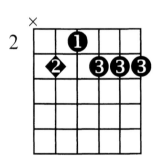

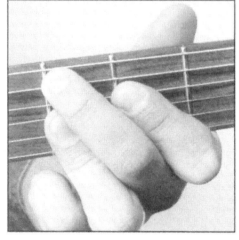

C m7

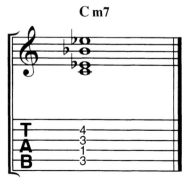

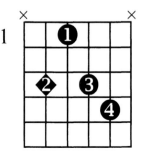

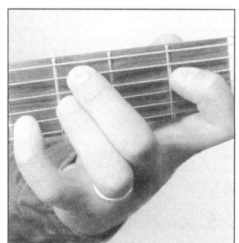

Note: the chords on this page are moveable and can be played
in any of the twelve keys. See page 24 for more information.

Other Moveable Chords

C m9

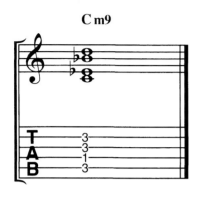

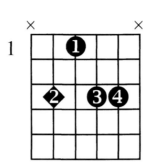

C m7(sus4)

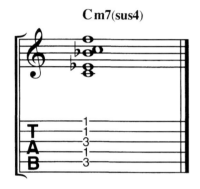

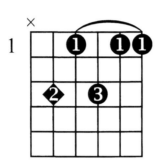

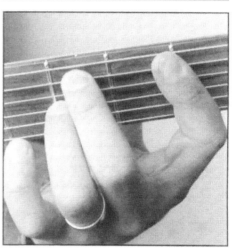

G 9

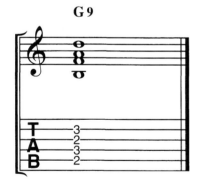

root not played

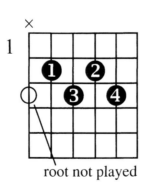

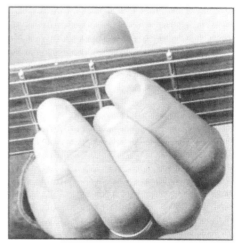

C 7(♯9)

The infamous
"Hendrix Chord"

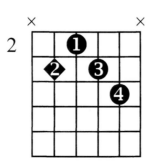

Note: the chords on this page are moveable and can be played
in any of the twelve keys. See page 24 for more information.

Other Moveable Chords

G sus4

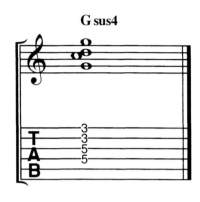

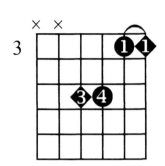

D 7

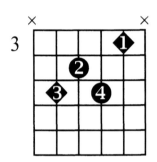

G 7

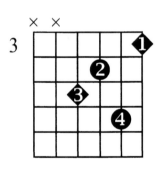

G Maj7

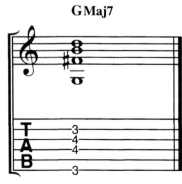

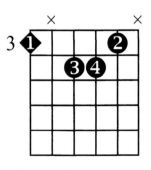

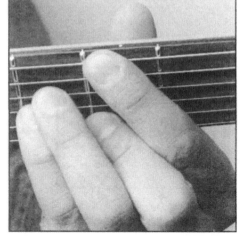

Note: the chords on this page are moveable and can be played in any of the twelve keys. See page 24 for more information.